Postcards
of
Hollywood's
Working Women

CAREER GIRLS

Selected by Michael Barson

Pantheon Books 🏛 New York

Introduction

Since the dawn of time, women have worked. Only recently, however, have they been *paid* for their labors. Does receiving pay for work equal having a career? Sure, if you do it long enough. (How about receiving *equal* pay? Next question.)

Nowhere has this been documented more vividly than in the American cinema, where women's entry into the workplace has been dramatized with unflagging invention. Remember Jean Arthur as the hard-boiled reporter in *Mr. Deeds Goes to Town*? Or Lucille Ball as *The Fuller Brush Girl*? How about Barbara Stanwyck as an evangelist in the 1931 film *The Miracle Woman*? Or Katharine Hepburn as a political columnist in *Woman of the Year*? Rosalind Russell practically made a career out of portraying career girls on-screen, in roles that included a literary agent (*What a Woman!*), a judge (*Design for Scandal*), a secretary (*Hired Wife*), an aviatrix (*Flight for Freedom*), a newspaper reporter (*His Girl Friday*), a psychiatrist (*She Wouldn't Say Yes*), and a college dean (*Woman of Distinction*). Though she did miss out on *Dance Hall Hostess*.

Sometimes just the titles of these films from Hollywood's Golden Age (i.e., anything dating from before Eddie left Debbie for Liz) tell the whole story: *Fashion Model* . . . *Convention Girl* . . . *She's in the Army* . . . *Hat Check Honey* . . . *Lady Gangster* . . . *Parachute Nurse* . . . *Timber Queen* . . . *Rosie the Riveter* . . . *Escort Girl* . . . the list goes on and on. (Today, of course, the cinematic choices have been narrowed down to *Escort Girl*, but that's another story.)

In this volume, you will find twenty-three stimulating professions for women which were glamorized in Hollywood films. While many of the titles—and even the actresses—might seem unfamiliar, there is little doubt that these humble movies were the stuff of myth that helped inspire yesterday's career girl to become today's career woman.

—Michael Barson, Director,
Career Girl Institute of Technology

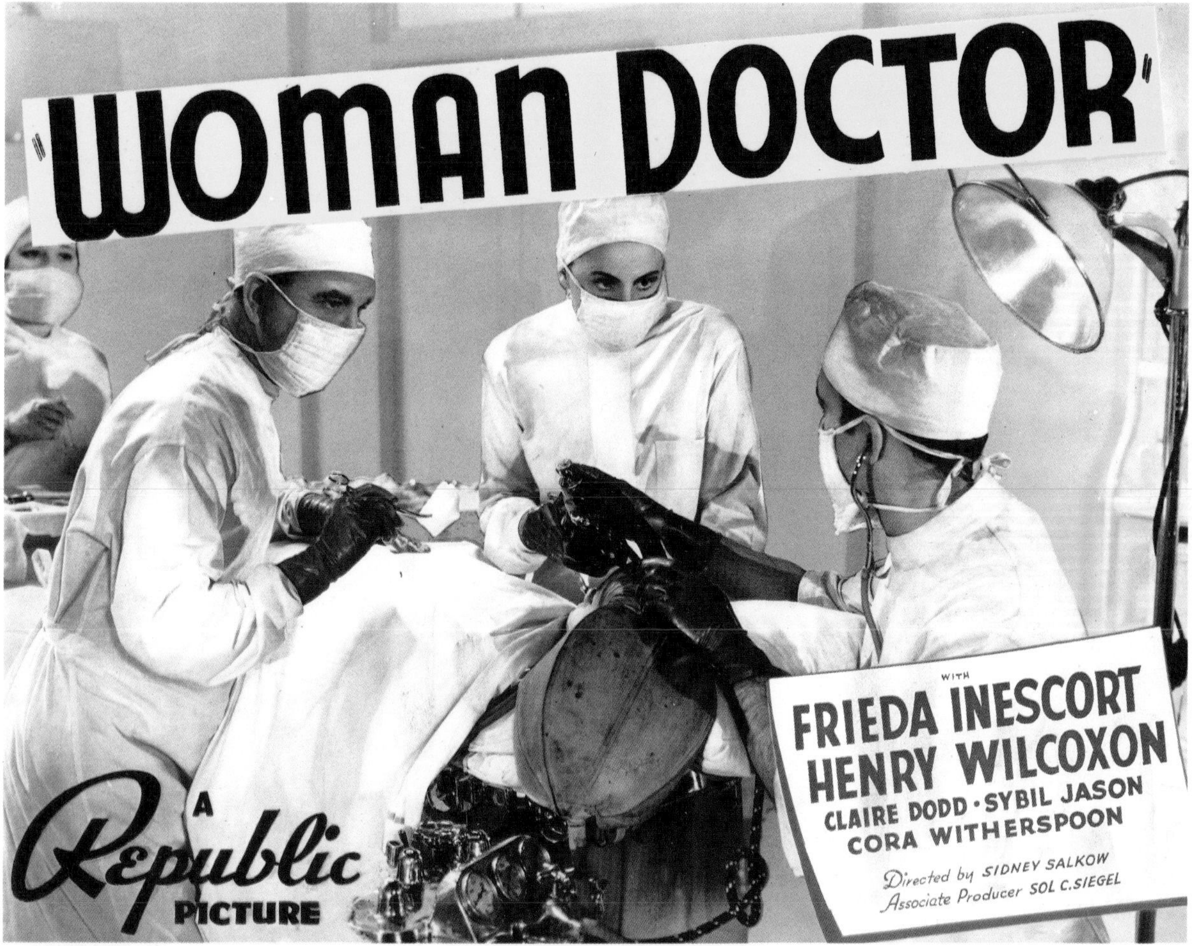
"WOMAN DOCTOR"
WITH
FRIEDA INESCORT
HENRY WILCOXON
CLAIRE DODD · SYBIL JASON
CORA WITHERSPOON
Directed by SIDNEY SALKOW
Associate Producer SOL C. SIEGEL
A Republic PICTURE

Woman Doctor (Republic, 1939) Another now-forgotten film from that legendary year 1939. This one featured Frieda Inescort, who presumably is conducting the operation from under that mask. The Scottish-born Inescort appeared on Broadway for several years before making her film debut in 1935. She was as likely to show up in prestige productions like *Pride and Prejudice* and *The Letter* as in lurid B's like *Convicted Woman,* all of which appear on her résumé for 1940. Kay Francis was *Dr. Monica* in 1934, and in 1952 June Allyson appeared in *The Girl in White,* the story of Emily Dunning, "New York City's first female doctor." The ad campaign boasted: "If men can do it, women can do it better"—wisdom we have seen proven time and time again.

from *Career Girls* • Pantheon Books • ed. Michael Barson • compilation and new text © 1989 Michael Barson

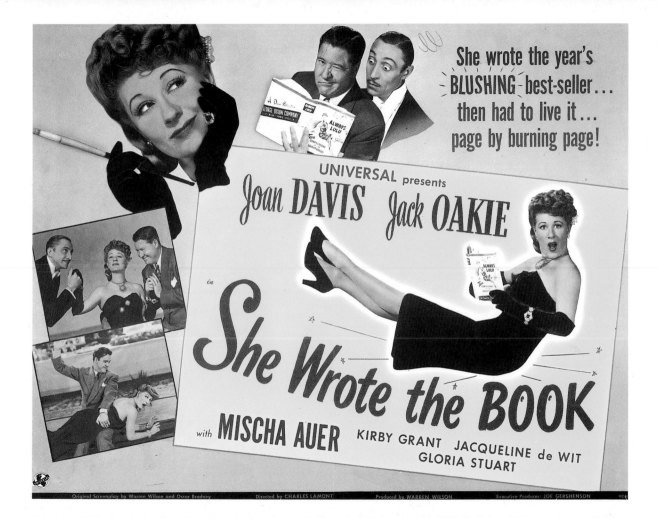

She wrote the year's
BLUSHING best-seller...
then had to live it...
page by burning page!

UNIVERSAL presents

Joan DAVIS   Jack OAKIE

in

She Wrote the BOOK

with MISCHA AUER   KIRBY GRANT   JACQUELINE de WIT
GLORIA STUART

Original Screenplay by Warren Wilson and Oscar Brodney   Directed by CHARLES LAMONT   Produced by WARREN WILSON   Executive Producer: JOE GERSHENSON

She Wrote the Book (Universal, 1946) Prim calculus professor Joan Davis is asked to impersonate the dean's wife (Gloria Stuart), who has written a steamy bestseller called *Always Lulu* that she's ashamed to promote. Davis goes to New York to begin the publicity tour, but a knock on the head scrambles her memory, and she now believes that she's led the lascivious life the book describes. Davis was a vaudeville veteran who livened up films like *Tail Spin* (as Alice Faye's wise-cracking mechanic) but really hit it big by producing and starring in the TV sitcom *I Married Joan* (with Jim Backus), which ran from 1952 to 1955. For more on bestselling authors in the movies, see Irene Dunne in the 1936 screwball classic, *Theodora Goes Wild*.

from *Career Girls* • Pantheon Books • ed. Michael Barson • compilation and new text © 1989 Michael Barson

"Saleslady"

WITH

ANNE NAGEL

A MONOGRAM PICTURE

Saleslady (Monogram, 1938) One can only imagine what Anne Nagel has on her mind as she attempts to sell a mattress to this over-enthusiastic gent, but it probably isn't her pension plan. Jean Arthur and Joan Crawford were among the stars who portrayed department-store clerks during their illustrious careers (in *The Devil and Miss Jones* and *Mannequin,* respectively). Nagel was in everything from the ''Green Hornet'' and ''Don Winslow'' serials, to B films like *Man-Made Monster* and *Women in Bondage,* but it was her 1939 programmer *Should a Girl Marry?* that speaks to today's career girls—or would, if anyone could ever see it.

from *Career Girls* • Pantheon Books • ed. Michael Barson • compilation and new text © 1989 Michael Barson

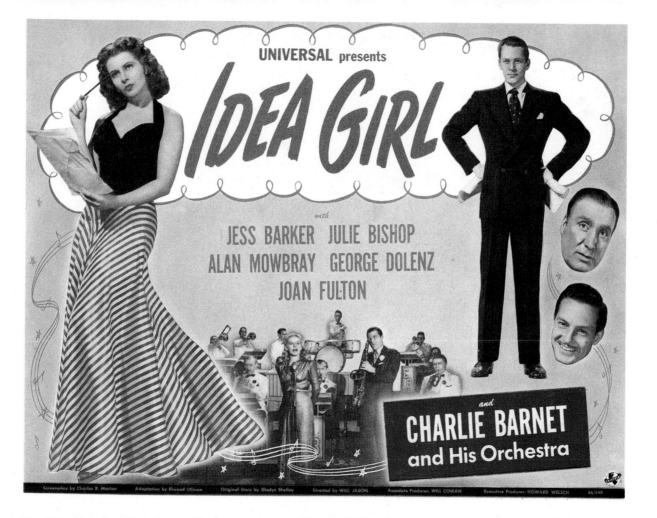

Idea Girl (Universal, 1946) Julie Bishop has to promote an amateur song contest for the publishing firm she works for, and you can see how it's made her brow furrow. But that's the world of PR for you: lotsa furrows, fewer ideas. Under the name Jacqueline Wells, Bishop appeared in the great Edgar G. Ulmer horror pic *The Black Cat* in 1934 and the evocative *Paid to Dance* in 1937, in which she was billed over the up-and-coming Rita Hayworth. Later, as Julie Bishop, she appeared in *I Was Framed, Lady Gangster,* and *The Sands of Iwo Jima.* Song-plugging never caught on in a big way as a career, and *Idea Girl* seems to be a Hollywood one-of-a-kind.

from *Career Girls* • Pantheon Books • ed. Michael Barson • compilation and new text © 1989 Michael Barson

"I fly because I need the money for my mother and my brother!"

"I fly because I love someone who thinks flying's the greatest thing in the world!"

"I fly because it's made me feel so close to things . . . and put me so close to my husband!"

Nancy **KELLY**

Constance **BENNETT**

Alice **FAYE**

TAIL SPIN

KANE **RICHMOND**

JANE **WYMAN**

CHARLES **FARRELL**

JOAN **DAVIS**

with
Wally Vernon · Warren Hymer · Joan Valerie · Edward Norris
Directed by Roy Del Ruth · Play by Frank Wead
Joe Brown · Original Screen Gordon & Ravel
Music and Lyrics by Pollack & Bullock
Associate Producer Harry in Charge of Production
Darryl F. Zanuck
A 20th Century-Fox
Picture

Three women of the sky! . . . the
heart-throbs behind their spectacular lives . . . the thrills that come
with their split-second escapes . . .
in a smashing romantic melo-
drama of adventure!

Every woman on earth will know
what's in their hearts—what makes
them take the gamble they can lose
only once!

Tail Spin (20th Century-Fox, 1939) Ah, the ups and downs in the life of an aviatrix. Alice Faye must win the Powder Puff High Speed Race to earn a lucrative job as a test pilot so she can support her mother and brother. But the competition is fierce, as rich-girl Constance Bennett has wings not unlike an X-15 built by her steel-baron daddy. Is there hope? Of course—Faye was Fox's #1 female star. Bennett throws the race to spite her boyfriend (Kane Richmond) and Faye lands the gig with the Sunbeam Oil Co. Also see Katharine Hepburn in *Christopher Strong*, Roz Russell in *Flight for Freedom*, a thinly disguised speculation on the disappearance of Amelia Earhart, and Anna Neagle in *Wings and the Woman*, a biopic about husband-wife pilots Jim and Amy Mollison.

from *Career Girls* • Pantheon Books • ed. Michael Barson • compilation and new text © 1989 Michael Barson

THE STARTLING EXPOSE

of beautiful models... and the Sordid Racket behind

MODELS, INC.

AND ALL ON THE MAKE... FOR FAME!

JACK DIETZ presents

HOWARD DUFF
COLEEN GRAY

in MODELS, INC.

$ BEAUTY FOR SALE

with JOHN HOWARD
MARJORIE REYNOLDS

Screenplay by HARRY ESSEX
and PAUL YAWITZ

Produced by REGINALD LE BORG

Directed by HAL E. CHESTER

Released by MUTUAL PRODUCTIONS CORP

Models, Inc. (Mutual Productions, 1952) When it comes to the modeling profession, Hollywood has always been of two minds. With Rita Hayworth in *Cover Girl,* Anne Shirley in *The Powers Girl,* Dorothy Lamour in *The Girl from Manhattan,* and Audrey Hepburn in *Funny Face,* the world of modeling has been portrayed as the ultimate glamor career. But then there's the other side—the side that suspects that, with all that dressing and undressing, *some*thing salacious must be going on. Sam Newfield's 1939 exploitation gem, *Secrets of a Model,* developed this theory in the cheeziest possible way, and *Models, Inc.* carried on the tradition by exposing one modeling operation as a front for a "party girl" service. Here Coleen Gray, whose career began with classics like *Kiss of Death* and *Nightmare Alley* and ended with *The Leech Woman,* goes undercover to help Howard ("Sam Spade") Duff rip the lid off this sordid enterprise.

from *Career Girls* • Pantheon Books • ed. Michael Barson • compilation and new text © 1989 Michael Barson

Night Waitress (RKO Radio Pictures, 1936) Fresh from her triumph as Katie the prostitute in the Oscar-winning *The Informer,* Margot Grahame somehow found herself stuck behind the counter in this crime-on-the-waterfront cheapie. Raised in white South Africa, Grahame was less than convincing as a dusk-to-dawn hash-slinger. As for the romance promised by the poster, it existed strictly in the fantasies of RKO's marketing department. The waitressing profession was more vividly rendered on-screen by Bette Davis in *Of Human Bondage,* Joan Crawford in *Mildred Pierce,* and Lana Turner in *The Postman Always Rings Twice.* (Crawford's 1945 Best Actress Oscar for *Mildred* was echoed thirty years later, when Ellen Burstyn won the award for her role as the waitress/singer in *Alice Doesn't Live Here Anymore.*)

from *Career Girls* • Pantheon Books • ed. Michael Barson • compilation and new text © 1989 Michael Barson

Robert L. Lippert presents

CESAR ROMERO

and

GEORGE BRENT

AUDREY TOTTER

in

RUPERT HUGHES'

FBI GIRL

"Woman..." on a man-hunt!

TOM DRAKE · RAYMOND BURR · Raymond Greenleaf · Margia Dean
Richard Monahan and introducing Tom Noonan & Pete Marshall
Screenplay by Richard H. Landau and Dwight Babcock
Produced and Directed by William A. Berke · Released by LIPPERT PICTURES, Inc.

FBI Girl (Lippert Pictures, 1951) Audrey Totter has been described as "a parboiled version of Alice Faye," which is a bit unkind but not inaccurate. She appeared in a number of good noirs, like *Lady in the Lake, Born to Kill, The Set-Up,* and *Tension,* and was never tougher than in *Women's Prison.* Here Totter is working to get the goods on an extortion gang, though she had a more interesting career-girl role in the 1947 film *The High Wall,* in which she's the police psychiatrist who helps clear Robert Taylor of a murder charge. Totter played a nurse on the *Medical Center* television series in the '70s, while fellow *FBI Girl* cast member Raymond Burr ended up as some kind of television lawyer, if memory serves.

from *Career Girls* · Pantheon Books · ed. Michael Barson · compilation and new text © 1989 Michael Barson

LOVE BRIDGES THE GULF BETWEEN A JUDGE AND AN UNDERWORLD GIRL!

A A A WOMAN IS THE JUDGE

ROCHELLE HUDSON

WITH FRIEDA INESCORT ★ OTTO KRUGER ★ SCREEN PLAY BY KARL BROWN · DIRECTED BY NICK GRINDE A COLUMBIA PICTURE

A Woman Is the Judge (Columbia, 1939) Frieda Inescort, last seen in *Woman Doctor,* is back as the judge in this B-grade morality play, but let's talk about co-star Rochelle Hudson instead, who plays the role of the girl in trouble. The reigning queen of the day's most sublime low-budget features (including *Convicted Woman, Missing Daughters,* and *Rubber Racketeers*), Hudson left films during the war to work alongside her husband in Naval Intelligence in Mexico and Central America. From convicted woman to real-life spy—good career move! Rosalind Russell appeared as a judge in the 1941 film *Design for Scandal,* just one more souvenir in her trophy case of career-girl roles.

from *Career Girls* • Pantheon Books • ed. Michael Barson • compilation and new text © 1989 Michael Barson

The
spectacular
rise
of a woman
in a man's
world

she
made good—
with a plunging
neckline, and
the morals of
a tigress.

SUSAN
HAYWARD

DAN
DAILEY

GEORGE
SANDERS

From
the most
startling
novel
of our
decade!

I Can Get it for You Wholesale

I CAN
GET IT
FOR YOU
WHOLESALE

A Novel by
JEROME WEIDMAN

20th CENTURY-FOX

with Sam Jaffe · Randy Stuart · Marvin Kaplan · Harry Von Zell · Barbara Whiting · Vicki Cummings · Ross Elliott · Richard Lane · Mary Philips

Directed by **MICHAEL GORDON** · Produced by **SOL C. SIEGEL** · Screen Play by Abraham Polonsky · Adaptation by Vera Caspary · From the Novel by Jerome Weidman

I Can Get It for You Wholesale (20th Century-Fox, 1951) "She made good—with a plunging neckline and the morals of a tigress." Susan Hayward is a designer who will stop at nothing to get ahead in this cynical tale of the New York garment industry. Hayward's tougher-than-thou style also served her well in the title role of *White Witch Doctor* and as Lillian Roth in *I'll Cry Tomorrow,* and let's not forget that she won the Best Actress Oscar of 1958 for her harrowing portrayal of accused murderess Barbara Graham in *I Want to Live!* For more celluloid on the designing biz, see Lauren Bacall in *Designing Woman,* Jane Wyman in *Lucy Gallant,* and Esther Williams in *Neptune's Daughter,* in which she designs—you guessed it—bathing suits.

from *Career Girls* · Pantheon Books · ed. Michael Barson · compilation and new text © 1989 Michael Barson

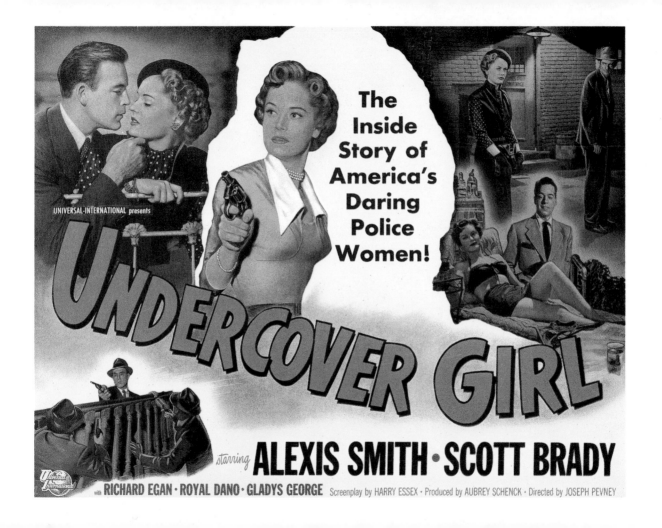

Undercover Girl (Universal-International, 1950) Alexis Smith joins up with
the police to track down the men who killed her father. Nothing special, but much more dignified
than, say, *Police Woman Centerfold*. Smith's heyday as an actress was the mid-'40s, when she was
a leading lady for Warner Bros. opposite the likes of Humphrey Bogart (in *Conflict*) and Cary Grant
(in *Night and Day*). She returned to film in 1975's *Jacqueline Susann's Once Is Not Enough* (so
titled to avoid confusion with *Marcel Proust's Once Is Not Enough*), thereby forfeiting her
policewoman's pension.

from *Career Girls* • Pantheon Books • ed. Michael Barson • compilation and new text © 1989 Michael Barson

Cafe Hostess (Columbia, 1940) "Where it's the man who pays and pays...or else!"
Thus has it ever been. Not to be confused with *Night Club Girl* or *Dance Hall Hostess,* this 63-
minute exposé went into release the same month as *Gone with the Wind.* Apparently the cafe racket
was less compelling than the plantation biz. Ann Dvorak had plum roles in such '30s classics as
Scarface (as Paul Muni's sister) and *G-Men* and *The Crowd Roars* (both with Jimmy Cagney), but had
to lower her sights later in the decade with such B exercises as *Girls of the Road* and *Gangs of New
York.* She also had the distinction of having Bette Davis steal George Brent from her in the 1934
film *Housewife.* No wonder she entered the work force.

from *Career Girls* • Pantheon Books • ed. Michael Barson • compilation and new text © 1989 Michael Barson

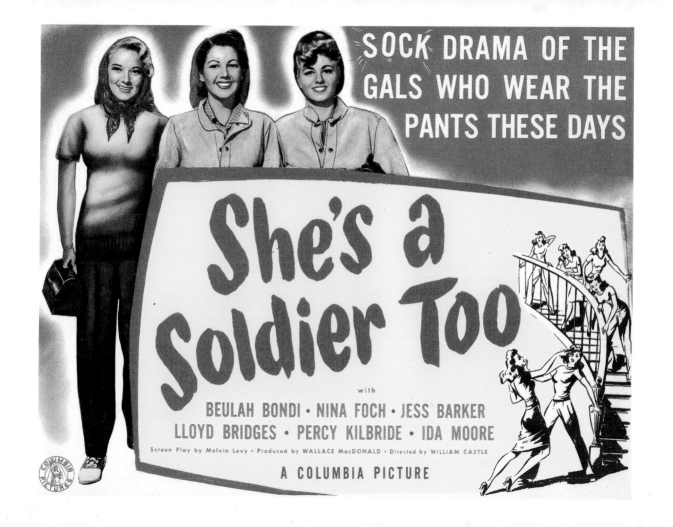

She's a Soldier Too (Columbia, 1944) A bunch of war-plant workers move into a Philadelphia mansion owned by Ida Moore and cabbie Beulah Bondi. The woman on the right is Shelley Winters, in one of her first roles. Other B films that celebrated the wartime contributions of working women include *Rosie the Riveter* and *Swing Shift Maisie,* in which Ann Sothern leaves the chorus line to work in an airplane factory. Star Veronica Lake clipped her trademark peekaboo locks around this time to set an example for women working in defense plants, some of whom had been getting their hair caught in the machinery.

from *Career Girls* • Pantheon Books • ed. Michael Barson • compilation and new text © 1989 Michael Barson

Smart about everything....except men!

ALLIED ARTISTS PRODUCTIONS presents

BRIAN
AHERNE

CONSTANCE
BENNETT

BARRY
SULLIVAN

"smart woman"

with
MICHAEL O'SHEA • **JAMES GLEASON**

OTTO KRUGER • ISOBEL ELSOM • RICHARD LYON • SELENA ROYLE
Directed by EDWARD A. BLATT • Screenplay by ALVAH BESSIE, LOUIS MORHEIM and HERBERT MARGOLIS
Adaptation by ADELA ROGERS ST. JOHNS

PRODUCED BY **HAL E. CHESTER**

Smart Woman (Allied Artists, 1948) "How smart is any woman who has men on her mind?" asked the ads for this meditation on the conflict between love and career. Constance (*Tail Spin*) Bennett plays an attorney hired by her ex-husband, racketeer Barry Sullivan, to defend him and his hoodlum pals. It's an assignment she doesn't relish, but Sullivan threatens to harm Rusty, their young son, if she doesn't oblige. Fortunately, her defense of Sullivan is trounced in court by special prosecutor Brian Aherne, with whom she's fallen in love, and the gang is sentenced to a long prison term while Bennett contemplates a new beginning as Aherne's wife. That's one way to ease the sting of losing a case. *Adam's Rib,* the classic Hepburn-Tracy film about husband-wife lawyers on opposing sides of a case, came out the following year.

from *Career Girls* • Pantheon Books • ed. Michael Barson • compilation and new text © 1989 Michael Barson

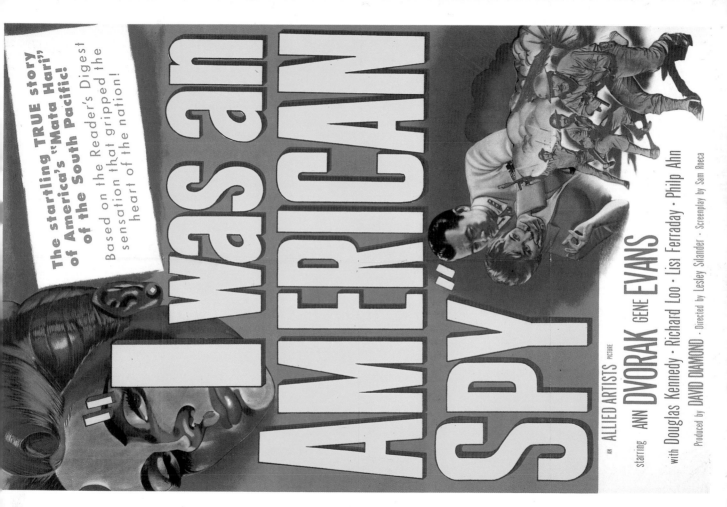

The startling TRUE story of America's "Mata Hari" of the South Pacific!

Based on the Reader's Digest sensation that gripped the heart of the nation!

"I was an AMERICAN SPY"

AN ALLIED ARTISTS PICTURE

starring ANN DVORAK · GENE EVANS

with Douglas Kennedy · Richard Loo · Lisa Ferraday · Philip Ahn

Produced by DAVID DIAMOND · Directed by Lesley Silander · Screenplay by Sam Roeca

I Was an American Spy (Allied Artists, 1951) Patriotic Ann Dvorak (seen earlier in this volume as *Cafe Hostess*) helps repel a Japanese attack on Manila during WWII. This was billed as the true story of America's Mata Hari, but the 1932 film with Garbo as the original, WWI-era spy is the more memorable. Hollywood was fascinated with spying as a profession for women, as indicated by films like *Madame Spy* with Fay Wray, *Operator 13* with Marion Davies, *Miss V from Moscow* with Lola Lane, *They Made Her a Spy* with Sally Eilers, and *My Favorite Blonde* with Madeleine Carroll, to name just a few. The early '50s was a popular time for the "I Was a…" approach to sensational subjects, and *I Was an American Spy* was joined at the box office by *I Was a Shoplifter* and *I Was a Communist for the FBI*.

from *Career Girls* • Pantheon Books • ed. Michael Barson • compilation and new text © 1989 Michael Barson

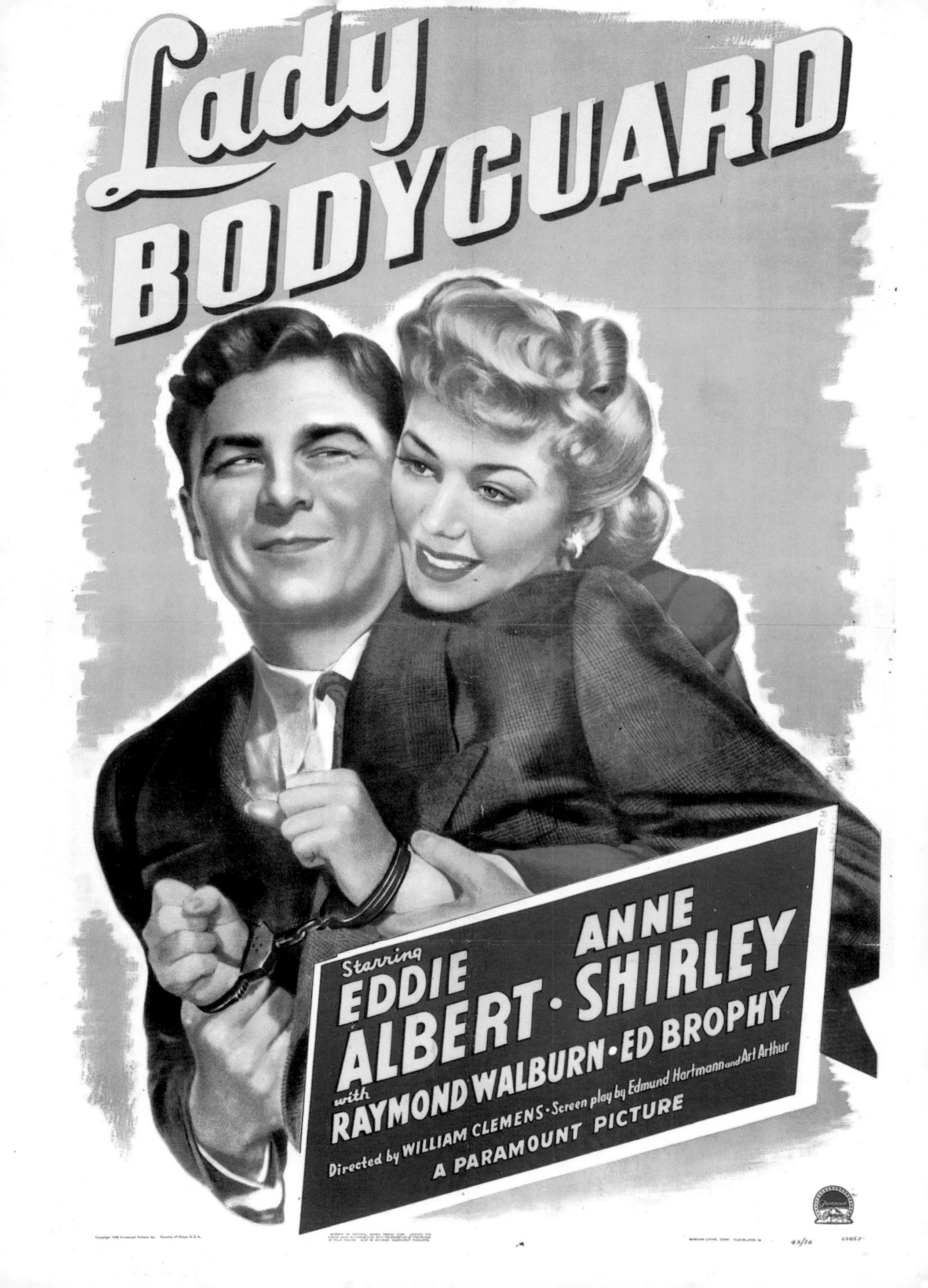
Lady
BODYGUARD
Starring
EDDIE ALBERT · ANNE SHIRLEY
with
RAYMOND WALBURN · ED BROPHY
Directed by WILLIAM CLEMENS · Screen play by Edmund Hartmann and Art Arthur
A PARAMOUNT PICTURE

Lady Bodyguard (Paramount, 1943) This real-life career girl began acting at age five, in silent films like *Riders of the Purple Sage* under the stage name "Dawn O'Day." As if her real name, Dawn Paris, wasn't just as exotic. Her role in *Anne of Green Gables* in 1934 inspired her newest name, Anne Shirley, which she appeared under in *Stella Dallas* (which earned her an Oscar nomination), *Boy Slaves, Music in Manhattan*, and the great noir *Murder, My Sweet*. She then married screenwriter Adrian Scott (an earlier marriage to actor John Payne ended in 1943) and retired from the screen. So did Scott—unwillingly, after being blacklisted as one of the Hollywood Ten.

from *Career Girls* • Pantheon Books • ed. Michael Barson • compilation and new text © 1989 Michael Barson

PRC PICTURES presents

Frances LANGFORD

IN

Career Girl

with

Edward NORRIS · Iris ADRIAN

CRAIG WOODS · LINDA BRENT
ALEC CRAIG · ARIEL HEATH.

Produced by JACK SCHWARZ ·· Directed by WALLACE W. FOX

Frances Sings
"Hey, That's How The Heat Began"
"Rhumba Day"
"Some Love Again"
"Blue In Came True"
"A Dream Came True"

PRC a Picture

Career Girl (PRC, 1944) Frances Langford was a perky big-band singer who enlivened such films as *Hit Parade of 1941, Cowboy in Manhattan,* and *The Bamboo Blonde* by appearing as— what else?—a big-band singer. Her only variation was to appear as an *aspiring* big-band singer in *Career Girl* (and of course she makes good). In the '40s, Langford had her own radio show, and even portrayed herself in the 1954 film *The Glenn Miller Story.* This was one career girl who didn't have to change her stripes. Doris Day, Betty Hutton, and Marilyn Maxwell were among the other big-band singers of the time who made the transition into films, Day enjoying the most success, even earning an Oscar nomination for Best Actress in the 1959 film *Pillow Talk.*

from *Career Girls* • Pantheon Books • ed. Michael Barson • compilation and new text © 1989 Michael Barson

PLACE
FIRST
CLASS
STAMP
HERE

Flight Nurse (Republic, 1953) First there was *Night Nurse* with Barbara Stanwyck. Then came *Registered Nurse, Prison Nurse, Nurse from Brooklyn, Private Nurse, Four Girls in White, Parachute Nurse,* and the biopics *Nurse Edith Cavell* and *Sister Kenny* (with perennial career girl Roz Russell). It would be nice to say that *Flight Nurse* represented the culmination of this noble genre —but the truth is, this was no more than a Korean War soap opera. As a child, Joan Leslie acted under her real name, Joan Brodel, then graduated to star status (and new name) in the early '40s in films like *High Sierra, Sergeant York,* and *Yankee Doodle Dandy,* alongside Bogart, Cooper, and Cagney. *Flight Nurse* co-star Forrest Tucker must have seemed quite a comedown.

from *Career Girls* • Pantheon Books • ed. Michael Barson • compilation and new text © 1989 Michael Barson